AUTHOR'S PREFACE

This little book is intended to introduce the reader to the joys of studying, keeping, and breeding the Ball Python, *Python regius*, which is one of the most popular snake pets in the world today. It is also an excellent snake to keep for those who no longer consider themselves beginners but instead have moved up onto a more intermediate level.

Today we find ourselves in a fortunate situation—many snake species, including the Ball Python, are being bred in captivity. This is important because many snakes (indeed, many reptiles overall) are still being killed for food, for skins, through sheer ignorance, or hunted and collected for the pet trade.

Another, probably more dramatic threat to many snake species, is the loss of habitat through man's continuing clearance of the world's wilderness areas, ostensibly for "improvement." Thus, keeping and breeding Ball Pythons in captivity is therefore a means of helping to preserve these fascinating creatures. And if this book helps that cause, then I will be more than satisfied.

John Coborn
Nanango, Queensland

The Ball Python, *Python regius*, is one of the most popular snakes in the herpetocultural hobby. Ball Pythons are attractive, easy to care for, and have a reputation for being fairly mild-tempered.

B. KAHL

INTRODUCING THE BALL PYTHON, *PYTHON REGIUS*

In the following chapter we will be looking at certain natural aspects of the Ball Python. Although the facts given are not essential for you to successfully maintain or even breed Ball Pythons in captivity, you should regard this information as background knowledge to your chosen hobby, which will surely enhance your enjoyment and lead you on the way to becoming a serious amateur herpetologist.

SUSAN C. AND HUGH MILLER

Ball Pythons are extremely heavy bodied, making them very powerful constrictors. Although they don't bite often, the bites they do give can be very painful, so beware.

BASIC FACTS

The Ball Python, *Python regius*, is a compact snake that averages about 4 ft/120 cm in length with occasional female specimens reaching 6 ft/180 cm or more. A large Ball Python would be 4 to 6 in/10 to 15 cm in diameter at the thickest part of the body (about halfway along its length). The head is narrow oval in shape and set distinctly from the body by a relatively narrow neck. There are

Facing Page: Unlike many other boids seen in the herpetocultural hobby, the Ball Python is relatively small, rarely growing over 6 ft/180 cm. This makes it considerably easy to manage, especially in regards to housing. Photo by Mella Panzella.

four distinct heat-receptor pits set in the first labial scales on either side of the upper jaw. The tail is relatively short.

The ground color is a light golden brown to creamy buff, which is broken by two, irregularly formed, chocolate brown, longitudinal stripes which are joined by crossbands at irregular intervals. The light-colored patches between the crossbands may have one or more chocolate brown blotches within their borders. The top of the head is chocolate-colored and bordered on each side by a light-colored stripe running from the snout to the neck. The underside is ivory white, with or without darker blotches or spots.

Ball Pythons are cold-blooded and thus must rely on their environment for bodily warmth. A wild Ball Python, for example, may live inside a hollow tree limb, the upper part of which is exposed to the sun all day (the warm part), the lower part being down in the shade (the cool part); and the snake just needs to move up or down as necessary. Of course, this system does not work at night and pythons would mainly be active at night only during the warmer

scales plays a major part in the snake's locomotion. Snake locomotion is a complex and

P. J. STAFFORD

Although known to most enthusiasts as the "Ball" Python, *Python regius* occasionally is called the "Royal" Python as well.

months (when temperatures stay over 68°F/20°C at night).

Ball Pythons are wholly carnivorous, taking prey compatible with their size. Due to their low metabolic rate, they do not require the food quantities needed by the higher animals, but a Ball Python will obviously take a substantial meal and then not eat again for some time.

MORPHOLOGY AND PHYSIOLOGY

The ventral scales of Ball Pythons are many times larger and broader than those on the rest of the body. This single row of large

interesting subject. Ball Pythons usually move with a combination of "snaking" and "rectilinear crawling." When snaking, the Ball Python advances by making a series of lateral curving motions, using solid objects such as stones, branches, tufts of grass, etc., for leverage with the rear part of the curves, in order to push itself forward. Because a snake needs to be very versatile in its body movements, it has a large number of sophisticatedly jointed vertebrae, each with an attached pair of ribs.

A Ball Python's sense of smell is

K. H. SWITAK

Closeup of the scales of a Ball Python. Note that they are smooth rather than keeled, and very shiny.

very highly developed and is closely involved with the two-pronged forked tongue that is continually flickering in and out through an opening (the labial notch) located at the front of the mouth. When the tongue is flickered out it picks up scent particles which are taken into the mouth and transferred to a pair of pits in the roof of the mouth. These are the openings to a very efficient sensing organ known as Jacobson's organ, which is literally for smelling the contents of the mouth. These openings are situated in the palate below the the nostrils but they form separate chambers lined with extremely sensitive membranes and work independently of the nasal sense of smell. The eyes of the Ball Python have vertical pupils, which is not unusual in nocturnal snakes. Other adaptations that probably occurred during a long-ago developmental period include a very acute sense of touch.

RANGE

The Ball Python occurs naturally in western Africa from Senegal in the north to Angola in the south, and westward through Zaire to Sudan and Uganda. It is probably at its most abundant in the West African rainforest areas from Ghana to Cameroon. Within its huge range it occurs in varied habitats from lightly wooded savannah to dense forest. Though it seems to favor the more open forests, it usually lives in areas where good cover is available. Being secretive, it likes to lurk in thick vegetation, among tree roots, or in boulder-strewn areas, always fairly near to permanent water. Though it is an adept climber, it spends most of its time on the ground, where it can best hunt its main prey of small burrowing mammals. During hot weather it occasionally bathes in water.

EVOLUTION AND CLASSIFICATION

Although snakes are thought to have evolved from burrowing lizards, there are no modern reptiles that show an intermediate phase, so the burrowing concept can only be regarded as theory until we can prove otherwise by finding the right fossils or by some other sophisticated means yet to be developed. In the meantime, we must continue conjecture about the true evolutionary story of our friend the Ball Python.

The Reptilia, the class to which the Ball Python and all other reptiles belong, is a group of vertebrate animals intermediate between the fishes and amphibians on one side, and the higher vertebrates (the birds and the mammals) on the other.

The Ball Python has the scientific name of *Python regius*, *Python* being the genus and *regius* being the specific part of the name. As there are also other species in the genus, these are given different specific names (for example: *Python molurus*, *Python reticulatus*, and *Python sebae*). In some cases a subspecific name may be added to the binomial, making it a trinomial. This is the case when

R. D. BARTLETT

The specimen shown represents a rather odd color variation of the Ball Python—notice the black stripe running along the vertebra. Such variations are rare in nature, but through selective captive-breeding they are often available to interested hobbyists.

two geographical races of a species are different but not different enough to warrant separate specific status.

Pythons form the subfamily Pythoninae in the reptilian family Boidae, which includes six more subfamilies: Boinae (typical boas); Bolyerinae (Round Island boas); Calabarinae (Calabar Ground Python); Erycinae (Rubber Boa, Rosy Boa, and sand boas); Loxoceminae (Mexican Dwarf Boa); and Tropidophinae (wood, or dwarf, boas). Perhaps the best way to view the position of the Ball Python in zoological classification is to look at a hierarchical table. We know that the python is an animal as opposed to a plant so we will start there:

Kingdom: Animalia (all animals)

Phylum: Vertebrata (Craniata) (all backboned animals)

Class: Reptilia (all reptiles)

Order: Squamata (lizards and snakes)

Suborder: Serpentes (all snakes)

Family: Boidae (pythons and boas)

Subfamily: Pythoninae (all pythons)

Genus: *Python* (typical pythons)

Species: *Python regius* (Ball Pythons)

DAVID DUBE

Unlike many other pythons, the Ball Python is not a great climber. It spends much of its time on the ground in search of small mammals. On particularly hot days, it may be found bathing itself in shallow waters.

HOUSING YOUR BALL PYTHON

Pet snakes are kept in a terrarium, vivarium, or cage, call it what you will. You must prepare the accommodations for your snakes before you get any specimens. There are no hard and fast rules concerning terrarium construction as long as the basic life-support systems are right. In the past, the standard type of terrarium was a glass-fronted box with an ordinary lightbulb. More recently, however, terrarium technology has advanced quite considerably. You can buy ready-made cages with all life support systems included. Such cages may be made from metal, fiberglass, or timber.

of juveniles until they are about 3 ft/90 cm long. Remember that snakes rarely stretch themselves out fully when resting and, if well-fed, will not be over-active. Also, regular handling sessions will ensure they get adequate exercise.

Of course, the tank has to have a secure but well-ventilated lid and it is best to make this a box structure, into which the heating and lighting apparatus can be installed. To protect the snakes from burns, the heating and lighting apparatus must be caged behind some strong metal mesh.

COURTESY OF HAGEN

Since Ball Pythons are of such a manageable size, finding a glass tank of appropriate dimensions certainly won't be a problem. Your local pet store will have many types for you to choose from.

The Glass Terrarium

Young Ball Pythons will be quite at home in a fish-tank full of air instead of water. A tank that is 3 ft x 1.5 ft x 1.5 ft/90 cm x 45 cm x 45 cm will be adequate for a couple

The Wooden Terrarium

As they grow, your Ball Pythons will require a somewhat larger cage. Many enthusiasts like to use timber terraria with glass viewing panels at this stage. Such cages are very versatile and can be made to a shape or size ready to fit into almost any corner. They can be free-standing, or constructed as a permanent fixture in an alcove. The glass access and viewing panels can be framed or unframed, hinged or sliding, but be sure not to leave any gaps through which snakes could escape. Even a fairly stout python can manage to

that will be suitable for them for the rest of their lives. A cage 48 in x 30 in x 36 in/120 cm x 75 cm x 90 cm would be suitable for a pair of adult Ball Pythons (bearing in mind that sexes should be kept separately for most of the year if breeding is to be successful). To make a really strong timber

DAVID ALDERTON

Needless to say, the more room you give your Ball Python, the happier the snake will be. Some keepers choose to build their own enclosures from scratch.

wriggle through a surprisingly narrow gap!

It often pays to be inventive, adventurous, and artistic when it comes to terrarium construction, and some ideal cages have been made from old closets, wardrobes, TV cabinets, and similar. A large display cabinet, for example, could easily be modified, maybe by a strengthening of the floor and attention to waterproofing. It is usually interesting to see what is available in your local "junk shop."

Once your Ball Pythons reach 3 ft/90 cm or more in length, it is best to construct a cage of a size

terrarium, the best material is undoubtedly 0.4 in/10 mm plywood. Chipboard, blockboard, or hardboard can also be used, but these are more prone to the effects of dampness than plywood and have to be treated with primer, undercoating, and at least two coats of good quality, non-toxic gloss paint for protection. Fiberglass resin is also an excellent waterproofer for such materials.

Terrarium Heating

Being strictly tropical, Ball Pythons will require supplementary heating in all areas outside the tropics for most of the year. The air temperature in the python cage should be maintained at 77 to 88°F/25 to 31°C during the day, reducing to 68 to 73°F/20 to 23°C at night. In most centrally heated homes, you will not require any additional supplementary heating in the terrarium at night, so you simply switch the heating apparatus off for the night and switch it on again in the morning. The day/night temperature cycle is important. It is bad for your snakes to be kept permanently at a constant high temperature; that is a mistake many budding keepers make. Get yourself a reliable thermometer so that you can monitor the temperature regularly,

Using a terrarium lining is a very sensible way to bed the enclosure of your Ball Python. Ranging in a variety of sizes, these linings are attractive, easy to work with, and can be used over and over.

It is important that a keeper of Ball Pythons closely monitors his or her snake's ambient temperature, so a reliable thermometer is advised. Since Ball Pythons naturally occur in a fairly warm region, it is essential that their temperature does not drop too low.

plus a thermostat to regulate the temperature automatically.

Many kinds of heating apparatus can be found on the market, but for the fish-tank terrarium as described above, ordinary domestic tungsten light bulbs can be used. You can experiment with wattages and a thermometer until you discover the right size bulb for your purpose, but a couple of 75-watt bulbs operated with a thermostat should be adequate for a tank of the size described. The bulbs should be installed in the box-lid, behind the wire mesh. They should be placed only at one end of the cage so that a temperature gradation is created from one end of the tank to the other. This will mean that a snake can move from warmer to cooler spots in the tank, and vice versa, to suit itself. If you need to apply some heat at night (such as when you keep your cage in an unheated garage or outhouse), you can produce warmth without creating excessive light by having a small wattage blue–or red-colored bulb, which is used at night only to keep the chill out.

In larger cages you will require more substantial heating. Large (150-watt plus) infra-red lamps and tubular steel heaters come to mind. It will pay to look around and see what is available. It is best to have all forms of heaters operated by a thermostat, and ensure that your Ball Pythons cannot get into direct contact with them. Some snakes have received severe burns by coiling around heaters.

Although the air temperature in your cages may be adequate for the snakes, they will soon chill if they enter a large volume of excessively cold water. Ideally, the water temperature should be 72 to 79°F/ 22 to 26°C day and night. Always add lukewarm water when replacing the bath water; the cage heater will then hopefully keep the chill out. Alternatively, you can use a thermostatically controlled aquarium heater, protected inside a plastic pipe which should be held under the water with a heavy brick or by some other means.

Lighting

Ball Pythons are naturally nocturnal, but they are still influenced by photo-period (the cycles of day and night). Their cages must therefore be ad-equately lit dur-ing the day. Several lighting manu-facturers produce fluorescent tubes that emit a so-called "day-light" or "broad-spectrum" quality of light. These can be used in conjunction with the heat lamps to provide excellent lighting. This is not to say full-spectrum lighting is *necessary* for a Ball Python's survival, but studies have shown that adult pairs generally fare better and have better breedings when subjected to a regular dosage of full-spectrum lighting.

COURTESY OF TETRA/SECOND NATURE

Heated blocks can be used to provide a Ball Python with bodily warmth. Since the heat is localized, the snake can move on or off the block whenever it chooses.

Ventilation

The importance of adequate ventilation in an enclosed terrarium cannot be over-stressed. It is essential for stale air to regularly be removed and replaced, remembering that such a process occurs naturally with wild snakes. You can ventilate the cage quite easily by having air vents located fairly low down in each end panel and a further one in the top. The convection currents caused by the heating will let stale air out from the top, being replaced with fresh air below. If you have adjustable vents that can be opened and closed as necessary, you will be able to control the airstream and prevent any excessively cold drafts.

Cage Furnishings

The simpler your cage furnishings are, the easier it will be to maintain good hygiene. Your pythons will require a floor covering, a water bath, a branch on which they can climb, and somewhere they can hide.

Paper towels or newspapers can be used as floor coverings for juvenile snakes and can be removed and replaced quite easily. The terrarium substrate for larger pythons can be shingle, which is changed and washed at regular intervals. Some hobbyists have made good use of artificial grass, bath towels, or old pieces of carpeting. By having a spare set of whatever you use, you can change it at regular intervals and wash the soiled ones so they are ready for next time.

As Ball Pythons do occasionally like to climb, a branch or group of branches should be provided. Such climbing facilities provide mental therapy, physical exercise, and an aid to shedding. The branches must be strong enough to support the snakes and must be secured to the floor and wall to prevent them from slipping.

Ball Pythons are generally secretive, which is why they like to squeeze themselves fairly tightly into hollows and cavities. In the wild they will use hollow limbs and branches, and root systems both on living and fallen trees.

COURTESY OF ENERGY SAVERS

Replicating correct photoperiods is an essential part of Ball Python keeping, particularly during the breeding season, when the changes in days and nights have a great effect on a snake's behavior.

COURTESY OF CREATIVE SURPRIZES

If you want to add a little visual spice to your Ball Python's tank, you should consider purchasing a piece of scenic sheeting, which can be attached right to a glass tank's back wall.

Sometimes they may take to rock crevices or the burrows of other animals. A cereal carton or shoe box (which can be changed when it gets grubby) is quite satisfactory as a hiding place, but may not be very esthetic. Some enthusiasts may use something similar to a parakeet nest-box, with a movable lid so that they have easy access to the snakes. A hollow branch is probably the most attractive and practical option. Choose one that has a large entrance hole on one side, but with a cavity through which the snake cannot squeeze completely out of sight.

A lighted hood will cast an attractive glow into any glass tank, and the flip-top lid makes it easy to offer food. Such hoods come in a variety of sizes and can be found at most any pet store.

COURTESY OF HAGEN

FEEDING BALL PYTHONS

There are a few reports about what wild Ball Pythons eat, and those that exist usually say that they eat small rodents. In their West African native habitat this very likely is true, but chances are they also probably opportunistically take other prey such as nestling birds and so on.

Ball Pythons are generally quite secretive and move under cover, and most prey is probably caught in burrows. The prey can be either the animals that made the burrows, or others that are there incidentally.

Since many prey animals are potentially dangerous, a Ball Python will use its efficient sense of touch and its coils to maneuver the head of the prey into a position in which the prey cannot bite. When the prey is dead, the snake loosens its grip and begins to examine the prey with its tongue in order to locate the head. A Ball Python almost always starts swallowing at the head end of the prey as this seems to be the easiest way to get it down into the gullet.

Snakes are well-known for the fact that they are capable of swallowing prey several times

A common concern for most keepers is whether or not their pets are "good eaters." This is not a problem with Ball Pythons; they are generally very hardy.

DAVID DUBE

Be careful! Ball Pythons can be very violent when grabbing their prey, so it's best to keep your hands well away from the center of activity.

Many keepers like to offer their Ball Pythons a food item that has already been killed. Even if you do this, the snake may choose to constrict it anyway.

ISABELLE FRANCAIS, COURTESY OF BILL AND MARCIA BRANT

The process of constriction can be somewhat horrifying, and many keepers may find this a bit unpleasant to watch. When it comes to feeding, Ball Pythons are not known for gentleness.

Since Ball Pythons can be so aggressive during feeding time, it is suggested that you offer their food via forceps rather than from your fingers.

Mice are the food item most often offered to young captive Ball Pythons, rats being the item given to the large specimens. Shown here is a litter of "fuzzies," or mice whose hair has only recently grown in.

wider than their own heads. They have several special adaptations to help them do this. First, the lower jaw is not hinged rigidly to the skull but is attached by elastic ligaments that allow a huge gape when the jaw is virtually "unhinged." Secondly, the lower jawbones can move forward along the prey's body in order to drag it further into the mouth. Next, the front of the first on one side and then the other as the prey slowly disappears into the snake's gullet. Once the prey has been

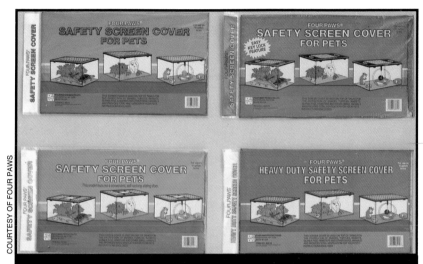

A screen cover is a sensible top to use when feeding Ball Pythons; it not only keeps the snake in the tank, but any live food items as well.

lower jawbones are connected with elastic tissue which enables the left and the right jaw to work independently of each other, allowing an enormous spread between them. In order to avoid damage to the brain while the python is swallowing large prey, the skull is totally enclosed in tough bone and is fairly mobile. Finally, the tissues of the gut, the flesh, and the skin are highly elastic to allow accommodation of large prey.

The snake begins to swallow once it has found the snout of the prey. If you watch this process, the prey seems to stay in one spot while the snake engulfs it, moving forward with its head and jaws over the prey's body, the lower jaws working

forced through the relatively narrow neck region, it is moved more speedily into the stomach.

After feeding, the Ball Python will need to rest for a few days to a week or more for digestion. The length of time will depend on the age and size of the snake (young snakes feeding more frequently), the size of the prey, and the prevailing temperature. It is important that temperatures are optimum during this time or digestion problems may otherwise ensue. At the higher part of the preferred temperature range, digestion will be quickest. In the wild, the snake will retreat into a sun-warmed refuge where it will rely on its camouflage to remain unnoticed by predators (including man).

Many enthusiasts breed their own food items for their snakes, but this tends to take up as much or even more time than tending the snakes themselves. Also, you would need to learn how to care for the food animal, bearing in mind that even if it is only "snake-food," it must still be kept in humane conditions! Let us look at some of the food items we may feed to our Ball Pythons:

Mice: Mice are available from pet shops and sometimes as surplus from medical laboratories. Some Ball Pythons do not take readily to mice at first but will usually do so after a certain amount of trial and error. Mice may be white or colored but that does not seem to make much difference as far as the snake is concerned. Some companies are now supplying bulk quantities of freshly killed and frozen mice which can be kept frozen until required. Allow a good 12 hours for the mice to reach room temperature before offering them. Do not thaw them by applying heat as this will change the composition of the flesh and also increase the risk of rapid decomposition which could

COURTESY OF FOUR PAWS

For added nutrition, some keepers like to use vitamin sprays, which can be utilized in conjunction with a number of captive reptiles.

continue in the snake's gut and make it sick. Baby mice are very suitable for juvenile Ball Pythons, whole adult mice will be taken by the snakes once they reach about 20 in/50 cm in length.

Rats: Rats can be obtained on a similar basis to mice. Ball Pythons can take young rats up to about half grown. Only a very large Ball Python should be given adult rats.

Chickens: Domestic fowl, up to a couple of weeks of age, can be used for Ball Pythons of various sizes. However, day-old chicks are not as nutritious as those which have been feeding for a few days, so day-olds should be fed in conjunction with mice or young rats. Bulk, deep-frozen chickens are also available in many areas. You may be able to obtain surplus live day-old chicks from your local hatchery and these can be kept and grown to sizes suitable for your snakes.

FEEDING STRATEGIES

It is difficult to say how often a python should be fed, but it is better to give it too little rather than too much. Once feeding on a regular basis, Ball Pythons are

R. T. ZAPPALORTI

Since adult Ball Pythons are such hardy animals, chances are they will only need to be fed once a week.

very prone to obesity, a condition in which many of the body organs become almost inoperative due to the enormous fat deposits in and around them. An obese python is unhealthy, will have a short life, and is not likely to breed!

A hatchling Ball Python will often not feed until after its first molt, up to one week after hatching. Young Ball Pythons should be fed on baby mice, or those that have just gotten their fur (these are called "fuzzies"). For the first three months you can give them maybe two mice a week as a start, but thereafter reduce to three a fortnight. When a ball python reaches about 2 ft/ 60 cm in length (at around six to eight months), it will graduate to adult mice and baby rats. One per week should be adequate; as the snake matures it will take larger rats and chickens.

FORCE-FEEDING

Occasionally a snake refuses to feed for no apparent reason, or it will refuse because it has or has had a disease. You must treat the snake for its sickness before or in conjunction with force-feeding (consult your veterinarian). There are two ways of force-feeding a Ball Python. The first is to take a whole dead prey animal (it is easier with a mouse or rat rather than with a chicken) of suitable size. Next take the snake by the neck and open its mouth by pulling gently but firmly at the loose skin under the jaw. When the mouth is sufficiently open, introduce the head of the prey animal and push it into the gullet as far as you can. Sometimes the snake will start swallowing on its own at this stage. If necessary, use something firm, but not too hard, like the lubricated (in mineral oil) handle of a wooden spoon to push the prey down toward the reptile's stomach. Once it is past the neck region you can usually massage the prey down into the stomach with your hand.

Another method of force-feeding is to use an instrument such as a large syringe to introduce liquefied food into the stomach. The stomach tube to which it is attached should have a smooth end and should be lubricated with mineral oil. You can also use a stomach tube thick enough to force down a whole mouse. The lubricated tube is passed slowly into the snake's gullet and the mouse is pushed down the tube with a plunger. Before you try any of these methods you are perhaps advised to obtain instruction from a veterinarian or a more experienced herpetologist.

Being such willing feeders, Ball Pythons rarely have to be force-fed, but when they do, it is advised the person doing the feeding has a second person to help them. Ball Pythons can be remarkably difficult to deal with when it comes to something like force-feeding.

K. H. SWITAK

When force-feeding any large snake, you must first grasp the snake's head firmly in one hand. If the head cannot be held still, the procedure will be very difficult. Specimen shown is a Burmese Python, *Python molurus bivittatus.*

MEDICAL ASPECTS

If you take proper care of your Ball Pythons and feed them on a healthy diet, they are unlikely to become sick. However, in the unfortunate event of a disease outbreak, it is advisable to be aware of what to do.

Prevention, of course, is infinitely better than trying to cure, and the key word to disease prevention is hygiene. Though the word hygiene is often related to sanitation, disinfectants, and chemicals, this is only a part of the science. The real basics of good hygiene are optimum environmental conditions.

Like all reptiles, Ball Pythons are unable to adapt to any climate that is substantially different to that which prevails in their original habitat. Being ectothermic, Ball Pythons must have an optimum temperature in which to operate. This is especially important during intake and digestion of food. A snake kept at too low a temperature will lose its appetite, and if it is kept at too low a temperature after feeding, its digestive processes will be inefficient. The food will only be partially digested in the gut and lack of digestive juices will allow putrefying organisms to attack the food, causing bloating, and maybe even toxicaemia.

If your Ball Python contracts a disease and you do not know what is wrong or how to deal with it, you will still need to consult a veterinarian. There is a whole new generation of veterinarians out there taking a greater interest in the more exotic pets and among them you will find those that are expert in reptilian diseases. Even if your local vet is inexperienced in snake medicine, he or she will be sure to be able to put you in contact with one who is.

The following is a brief list of the more common conditions and diseases that you may come across:

Malnutrition: This is not often a problem, as Ball Pythons are usually fed on animals that have been raised on a balanced diet. In cases of vitamin deficiency (due to feeding on nutritionally substandard day-old chicks for example), fluid vitamin/mineral supplement can be injected into a dead prey animal before feeding it to the snake. Your vet may occasionally recommend the introduction of concentrated nutrients and/or medicines to the stomach of a snake that is being treated for a disease. This will be administered via a

Facing Page: Keeping a Ball Python alive and well takes a lot of time, patience, and attention to detail. The snake will be dependent on you for every aspect of its captive care. If you are not willing to accept such a responsibility, then you should consider not having a Ball Python at all. K. H. Switak.

stomach tube.

Wounds and Injuries:
Though not strictly diseases, wounds are occasionally caused by fighting, attempting to escape, lamp or heater burns,

By denying a Ball Python its required vitamins and minerals, you will run into a whole mess of problems. In the photo shown, the snake depicted has been so lacking in proper nutrition, its skin has actually begun to break away from its body. Snake shown is a Boa constrictor, *Boa constrictor.*

DR. FREDRIC L. FRYE, IN *REPTILE CARE*

rodent bites, and so on. Such wounds are likely to become infected if not treated. A shallow wound will usually heal quickly if swabbed daily with a mild antiseptic such as povidone-iodine. Deeper or badly infected wounds should be dealt with by a veterinarian as in some cases surgery, suturing and antibiotic treatment may be required.

Ectoparasites: Mites and ticks are the most usual blood-sucking ectoparasites (living outside the body) associated with snakes. A mite infestation can be regarded as serious, as mites can often multiply to large numbers in the terrarium before they are even noticed. They do not stay on the reptiles's bodies all of the time but hide in crevices in the terrarium, coming out at night to suck blood through the softer skin between the scales. In great numbers, mites can cause stress, shedding problems, anemia, loss of appetite, and eventual death. They are also capable of transmitting blood-pathogenic organisms from one reptile to another. The individual reptile mite is smaller than a pinhead, roughly globular in shape, and grayish in color, becoming red after it has taken a blood meal. In a heavily infested terrarium, the mites may be seen running over the surfaces, particularly in the mornings, and their tiny, silvery, powdery droppings may be seen on the pythons's skins. Mites are most often introduced into the terrarium with new stock (another good reason for quarantine and careful

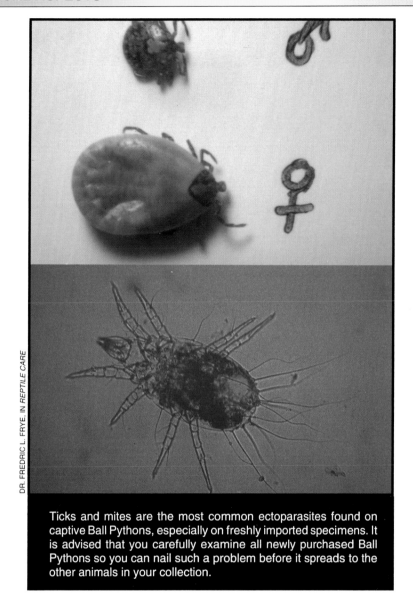

DR. FREDRIC L. FRYE, IN REPTILE CARE

Ticks and mites are the most common ectoparasites found on captive Ball Pythons, especially on freshly imported specimens. It is advised that you carefully examine all newly purchased Ball Pythons so you can nail such a problem before it spreads to the other animals in your collection.

inspection).

Mites can be quickly eradicated using an insecticidal dichlorvos strip (of the type used to control houseflies). A small piece of such a strip placed in a perforated container and suspended in the terrarium will kill off free-moving mites. Remove the strip after three days then repeat the operation ten days later to kill off any newly hatched mites. Two or three treatments will usually destroy all mites in the terrarium. Do not allow your pythons to come into direct contact with the actual insecticidal strip.

Ticks are often found attached to newly captured reptiles, though they are rare in

DR. FREDRIC L. FRYE, IN *REPTILE CARE*

Ticks can be seen with the naked eye fairly easily, but mites are so tiny that they will have to be searched for. A mite infestation in its early stages can be cured without too much trouble but one that is left unattended to can cause a snake great harm, possibly even death.

captive-bred Ball Pythons. Ticks range up to .25 in/5 mm in length. They fasten themselves with their piercing mouthparts to a snake's skin, usually in a secluded spot between scales, often around the vent or under the chin. Do not attempt to pull a tick directly out as its head may be left embedded in the skin, causing further infection later on. The tick's body should first be dabbed with a little alcohol (surgical spirit, meths, or even a drop of rum) to relax the mouthparts. The tick can then be gently pulled out with forceps or even with the thumb and forefinger.

Endoparasites: The most abundant kinds of endoparasites (living inside the body) in snakes are various species of intestinal worm, the most common being types of roundworms and tapeworms. Nearly all wild snakes are infected with worms of one form or another, but, in most cases, there is no danger to the reptiles. However, during times of stress (capture, unsuitable heating, starvation, other diseases, for example), normal resistance to the worms may be reduced, triggering a massive increase in size or numbers of worms, causing anemia, general lethargy, loss of appetite, and eventual death. Routine microscopic examination of fecal samples in a veterinary laboratory will reveal infestations. There are several proprietary brands of vermicides available through your veterinarian which may be offered with the food or, in severe cases, via stomach tube.

Skin Problems: The most frequent types of skin problems to occur in pythons arise as a result of inadequate shedding, which itself occurs often as a result of a mite infestation or

DR. FREDRIC L. FRYE, IN *REPTILE CARE*

Improper shedding can turn into a real problem for a snake if left untreated. In mild cases, an eye cap may stick to an eye and infect the entire region; in more severe cases, blindness can result. Snake shown is a Boa constrictor, *Boa constrictor.*

stress brought about by various other factors. Mite infestations should be cleared immediately and aid should be given to snakes experiencing difficulty in sloughing. Most healthy pythons will slough (molt) their skins without problems several times per year. It is a natural process related to growth. The skin is normally shed in a single piece and the whole procedure should take no more than a few hours. Unhealthy skin caused by various factors may result in the skin coming away in patches. Disease organisms can grow behind persistent patches of old skin which do not come off readily, and these can infect the skin beneath, resulting in lesions or other unpleasant disorders if untreated. The skin can be loosened and peeled off by placing the reptile in a bath of very shallow warm water for an hour or so.

Other infections of the body surface include abscesses, which appear as lumps below the skin. These are usually caused by infection building up

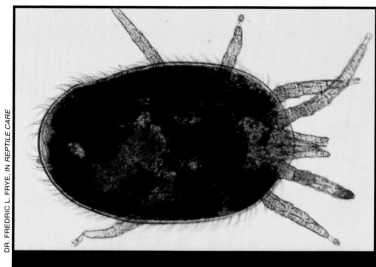

DR. FREDRIC L. FRYE, IN REPTILE CARE

Unless a mite infestation has grown completely out of control, a keeper should be able to eradicate it with the help of a small piece of pest strip.

in the flesh after the skin has been accidentally damaged for one reason or another. Abscesses should be referred to a veterinarian, who will give antibiotic treatment. In severe cases the abscess may be surgically opened, cleaned up, and then sutured.

Eye Problems: Because the eyes of snakes are protected by the transparent spectacle, eye diseases are relatively rare. However, a condition known as pop-eye occasionally arises, in which fluid builds up in the eye below the spectacle, causing the latter to swell up out of proportion. Do nor attempt to burst the spectacle, but refer it to a veterinarian.

Another problem that occasionally arises is that the skin of the spectacle remains unshed, especially after a difficult shedding. In severe

cases, two or more old skins may cover the spectacle, rendering the snake almost blind. The skin should be loosened by bathing the snake in lukewarm water for several minutes, then drying with a cloth and attempting to remove the skin with a piece of sticky tape. Do not use a sharp instrument as there will be a danger of damaging the spectacle. Difficult cases should be referred to a veterinarian.

Respiratory Infections: Though relatively uncommon in pythons, respiratory infections may occur occasionally in stressed specimens. The affected python will have difficulty in breathing, the nostrils will be blocked and there will be a nasal discharge. Often the symptoms can be alleviated by moving the sick reptile to a warmer, drier, well-ventilated terrarium. More serious cases should be referred to a veterinarian, as antibiotic treatment may be required.

Protozoan Infections: A number of intestinal infections can be caused by protozoa, the best known probably being amoebiasis caused by *Entamoeba invadens*. Untreated, such diseases can rapidly reach epidemic proportions in captive reptiles.

Symptoms include slimy, watery feces and general enervation. Treatment with metronidazole (by a veterinarian) via stomach tube has proved effective for this and other protozoan infections.

Bacterial Infections: A wide variety of enteric bacterial diseases can infect pythons. Infective salmonellosis is an intestinal disease which has been known to have been

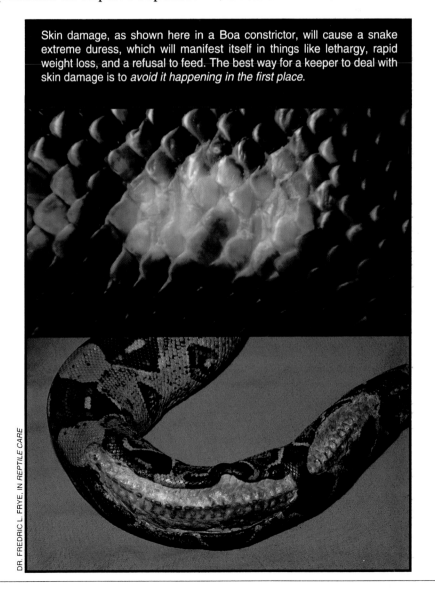

Skin damage, as shown here in a Boa constrictor, will cause a snake extreme duress, which will manifest itself in things like lethargy, rapid weight loss, and a refusal to feed. The best way for a keeper to deal with skin damage is to *avoid it happening in the first place.*

DR. FREDRIC L. FRYE, IN *REPTILE CARE*

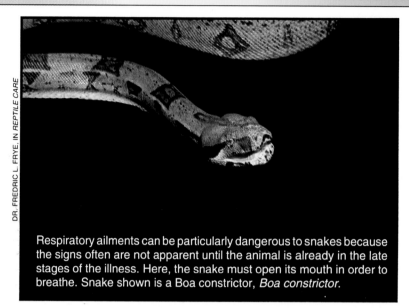

DR. FREDRIC L. FRYE, IN *REPTILE CARE*

Respiratory ailments can be particularly dangerous to snakes because the signs often are not apparent until the animal is already in the late stages of the illness. Here, the snake must open its mouth in order to breathe. Snake shown is a Boa constrictor, *Boa constrictor*.

transmitted from reptiles to man (especially from freshwater turtles) so it is important to thoroughly wash your hands after each cleaning or handling session. In pythons, salmonellosis manifests itself in the watery, green-colored, foul-odored feces. Consult a veterinarian who will probably treat the infection with an antibiotic drug.

When a snake has become bloated to this extent due to a respiratory problem, its chances of recovery are slim. Respiratory illnesses are often the result of keeping a snake far below its normal temperature.

DR. FREDRIC L. FRYE, IN *REPTILE CARE*

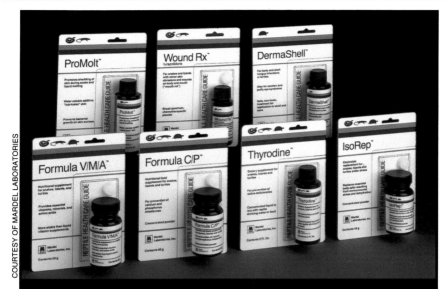

COURTESY OF MARDEL LABORATORIES

Preventive medicine is the only form of reptile medicine an ordinary keeper should practice. There are a number of products you can purchase designed to help you with such an endeavor, seven of which are shown here.

Shedding is a normal part of a snake's life, but a bad shed can cause real problems if not attended to. A snake going through a shed cycle should always have water to bathe in (to soften the old skin) and a rough surface, like a rock, on which to begin the shed.

ROBERTA KAYNE

BREEDING BALL PYTHONS

The growing concern for the earth's disappearing wilderness areas and the accompanying threat to the continuing existence of many forms of wildlife should make every keeper of exotic creatures all the more determined to get his or her animals to reproduce. Many species are now almost impossible to obtain from the wild due not only to their increasing scarcity, but also to international protective legislation. Unfortunately, a certain amount of reptile smuggling still goes on, and this makes prices artificially high. Keepers of particular species such as Ball Pythons have a duty to keep captive stocks at a level that will meet demand, to discourage smuggling and keep prices at a reasonable level. Since herpetological interests are likely to continue to increase, there is every reason to believe that the demand will be greater in the future; all the more reason for sustained captive-breeding.

An unfortunate aspect of captive-breeding with such animals, and one that gives us a certain amount of concern, is the fact that the relatively small captive gene pool has given rise to increasing anomalies that may be very interesting for the geneticist, but are not really esthetically desirable. While I am not totally against color breeding if applied in a sensible manner, I would really hate to see the morphology of snakes, including Ball Pythons, manipulated genetically as has been done, for example, with dogs, many of which bear little or no resemblance to how they evolved naturally. For this reason it is important that sooner or later we must try and initiate a pedigree system for various species. Studbooks would make a good start and we should try and keep strict records of our breeding results for the benefit of all python breeders now and in the future.

Ball Pythons reach sexual maturity not necessarily with age but with size. Males are ready to breed when about 2 ft 6 in/75 cm, and females when about 3 ft/90 cm in length. Well-fed hatchlings will reach these sizes in about two years, but for better results it is recommended that the snakes are fed moderately so that they do not become obese in their younger stages and reach the size for sexual maturity in three to four years.

It is thought that, in the wild, humidity, moderate lowering of temperature, and possibly seasonal atmospheric pressure changes all have a direct influence on the sex drive of Ball Pythons, and mating takes

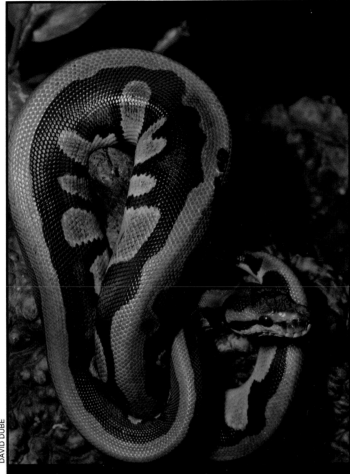

DAVID DUBE

The art of captive-breeding has skyrocketed in popularity over the last decade. Now, thanks to the efforts of some very talented herpetoculturists, unique specimens, like this stunning gold-striped Ball Python, are available for show or sale.

place at the beginning of the wetter seasons which are mainly in the early summer months in the natural range of the pythons. The main habitats of the Ball Python in these areas are open woodland to dense forest, usually close to permanent water. There is a short dry season in the rainforest areas, being slightly longer in the savannah regions. In the summer, temperatures are usually well above 70°F/ 21°C and rainfall is monsoonal in some parts of the range. The timing of mating and egglaying is such that the young will hatch at a climatically favorable time, when it is warm and moist and there is an abundant supply of food prey which will give the juveniles a good start in life.

The prospect of breeding your Ball Pythons is, to most

The best adults to use as breeding stock are those who themselves have been captive-bred and raised. They will generally be much calmer and thus more amenable to captive living.

fanciers, the the most exciting aspect of the hobby. However, it is only snakes that are completely healthy and given the necessary stimuli that will court and mate. Our knowledge of wild habitats is of great assistance to us with regard to providing the right conditions.

SEX IDENTIFICATION

A very obvious requirement for breeding your pythons is that you must have one of each sex! In adult Ball Pythons, the the male is shorter (to 4 ft/120 cm maximum) and generally more slender in form, while the female is longer (to 6 ft/180 cm maximum) and generally more robust in form. In well-fed snakes, it is quite easy to distinguish the sexes from about six months of age. However, it is not quite so easy with juveniles under 18 in/45 cm in length. This is best done with a sexing probe. The lubricated metal probe (available from specialist suppliers) is inserted into either side of the vent and pushed very gently toward the tail tip. In females, the probe can only be pushed the distance of three subcaudal scales or less, but in males the probe will enter the sulcus (the sac at the base of the tail that contains the inverted hemipenis) and can be pushed the equivalent of about ten subcaudal scales toward the tail tip. Great care must be taken to ensure no damage is done to the fragile internal tissues, and you are advised to take instruction in the probing procedure from somebody who is experienced in the process before attempting it yourself.

BRINGING THE SNAKES INTO BREEDING CONDITION

Wild Ball Pythons are fairly solitary outside the breeding season and will therefore usually ignore chance meetings with the opposite sex. There is evidence to suggest that keeping the sexes separate until breeding time will increase chances of successful breeding. You are therefore advised to keep your males and females separated. A good time to introduce a female to a male is just after the female has shed her skin when the more intense smell of the

Techniques for captive-breeding snakes have developed greatly over the last decade. Ball Pythons are among the most often captive-bred snakes, which is good news for both the environment (which does not suffer depletion of its own stock), and the interested hobbyist (who will receive first-rate specimens).

R. APPLEGATE

pheromones on the fresh skin is likely to stir him into sexual activity.

Ensure your snakes are well fed throughout the year and, when you require a breeding response (which can be at any time of the year but summertime is perhaps most effective) start decreasing the light intensity and temperature in the cage. Over a period of about six weeks, gradually reduce your maximum daytime temperature down about eight degrees. Introduce females to males toward the end of your temperature reductions, preferably when a female has just shed, and you should get an almost immediate mating response. The female snakes will have been affected by the environmental change and will have started to release vitellogin pheremones (sexual attractants) from areas between the scales. This pheromone is sweet smelling to the male snake and should sexually arouse him to the extent that he wants to copulate with the female.

MATING

The male will approach the female and crawl along her back, with much jerking of his body and massaging with his cloacal claws. At the same time his tongue will be flickering in and out rapidly as he smells her pheromones. Eventually he gets into a position where he can push the rear part of his body under hers so that he can get his cloaca into apposition with hers. If the female is receptive she will make it easy for the male to insert one of his, now erect, hemipenes into her cloaca. Copulation can take anything from a few minutes to several hours. During this time the snakes usually remain still while the sperm transfers from male to female.

After the sexes separate, the male can be left with the female for a week or so at the reduced temperature to allow any successive matings, in case the first one was infertile. After a couple of weeks, the male should be moved back to his own cage and you should again start to increase the temperature.

THE GRAVID FEMALE

The fertilized female is said to be *gravid*, and her eggs will start to develop. She will keep the eggs in her body for 50 to 120 days, usually about 60 to 70 days. After about 25 days of gravidity, the rear end of the female's abdomen takes on a plump appearance, and later the actual outline shape of the eggs can be seen along the body. The snake will usually stop feeding after about the third week of gravidity, and will not feed again until the eggs hatch. A gravid snake should be handled as little as possible.

EGGLAYING

When ready, the female will lay her eggs somewhere on the cage floor, often in the hidebox.

The incubation of snake eggs is a delicate affair. Here, a clutch of eggs is incubating on a bed of moistened sphagnum moss. The blue line is attached to a monitor for temperature and humidity.

The elongate eggs are about 3 in/7.5 cm long (relatively large for the size of the snake), with a soft, white, leathery shell, and usually about three to eight in number. They are pushed together into a pile by the female, and she coils around them, fully covering them with her body. It is best to allow the female to guard the eggs herself, rather than take them away for artificial incubation. It is important to maintain a daytime temperature of 86 to 90°F/30 to 32°C at this time, reducing to about 77°F/25°C at night. If artificial incubation is necessary, you will require a simple incubator. The eggs should be placed in moist vermiculite and incubated at 86 to 90°F/30 to 32°C. It is important to maintain a high humidity (by mist spraying) during incubation, whether natural or in an incubator, although be careful not to spray the eggs themselves.

Pythons that perform their own incubation are unique in the reptile world in being able to elevate their body temperature above that of the surrounding environment, by physical means. During incubation, the snake's muscles twitch regularly, and this is related to the snake's ability to raise its temperature. Though it is thought to be much less proficient at raising its temperature than some of the larger species, the Ball Python is usually a good mother, sometimes leaving the eggs to bask and warm up, returning to transfer some of the warmth to the eggs.

Incubation takes 80 to 105 days. Often not all of the eggs will hatch; some may have been infertile while others may have stopped developing somewhere along the way, but you should expect 50 to 80% success. The mother will leave the eggs and return to her routine method of living as soon as they begin to hatch and will show no further interest in her young. Allow each youngster to fully emerge from its egg before moving it to a separate cage.

REARING

The young will not feed until after the first molt, which is usually two to eight days after hatching. They are about 12 in/30 cm in length and should be fed on baby mice or gerbils. For the first few months, one mouse per week should suffice, increasing the size of the rodent as the snake grows. Do not overfeed and cause fast growth, because this can lead to obesity. Young pythons should be tamed by frequent and regular handling (but not on feeding day or the day following).

Facing Page: Ball Pythons are not uncommon on the pet market, so getting your hands on a choice specimen will not be difficult; the Ball Python has been captive-bred through many generations and specimens are usually quite affordable. Shown is a beautiful golden-striped variety. R. D. Bartlett.

MISCELLANEOUS TOPICS

ACQUISITION

Having made the decision that Ball Pythons are your pet of choice, do not impulsively buy the first one you see. You will already, hopefully, have considered all aspects of python keeping and have prepared suitable accommodations with life support systems that work reliably.

You may acquire a python in one of several ways, the most probable being from a pet shop or from a specialist reptile dealer. Since Ball Pythons have grabbed the attention of the herpetocultural community, the availability of top-quality specimens is rather high. Most are reasonably priced and will adapt quickly to captive life, which is good news for any Ball Python enthusiast

It may be worth first looking around for a few days to see what is on the market. Be careful dealing with shops that are untidy and dirty and have unhealthy looking specimens in smelly, overcrowded cages. Unfortunately there are still a few such premises about, although modern hygiene and animal welfare legislation in most countries are tending to get them cleaned up. Most of our modern dealers have spotless, professionally kept premises

and take pride in presenting their stock in clean, attractive display cages. Such dealers are always keen to answer any specific questions you may have with regard to the future care of any stock you may purchase.

However, before purchasing your python, you should give it a careful examination to ensure that it is fit and healthy. Make sure there are no external parasites such as ticks or mites on the snakes or in the cage. Ensure that the reptile is clear-eyed, plump, and alert, not dull-eyed, emaciated, or lethargic. Look for signs of inflammation around the mouth that could indicate mouth-rot. Avoid specimens that do not show interest in your handling by tongue flickering, movement, and possible struggling (the latter in the case of snakes that are unaccustomed to regular handling). Ensure the snake has no genetical defects such as a spinal kink, a deformed eye, or aberrant scalation. Such defects could be passed on when the snake breeds and the resulting aberrations in the offspring could be even worse.

You will, of course, need to handle the snake when

Facing Page: Although Ball Pythons are generally calm and trustworthy, you should not make it a practice to drape them around your neck. Small children are particularly susceptible to injuries when performing such acts. Isabelle Francais.

inspecting it. If you are not yet confident about snake handling, it will be best to take someone who is when you go to the dealer. The dealer would probably show you how to handle a snake, but it is better that you are able to act independently when you are purchasing.

Another thing you must do when acquiring a new python is to find out if it is feeding and on what. It may, for example, have been feeding on gerbils because it is not a good mouse eater. It is important that you know these facts in order to plan your feeding strategies.

TRANSPORTING YOUR PYTHONS

The most satisfactory method of carrying snakes, and one that has been used for many years, is to pack the reptiles individually in cloth bags. The snakes feel secure in the soft folds of the bags and can get adequate air through the cloth. Specially made bags of strong cotton, drill, or linen are ideal, but strong pillow cases or rice sacks will usually do quite well. The serious enthusiast will always have a selection of bags of various sizes. Always try to have small bags for juvenile snakes. Never place a bag on a raised surface such as a chair or table, as the snake, moving inside the bag, could fall off and injure itself. A number of snakes in separate bags can be packed in partitions in large wooden, or thick cardboard, transport boxes. If the box has to travel during excessively cold weather it should be lined with an insulating material. Always select the quickest and most direct route of dispatch.

When purchasing new stock, it is always best to pick it up yourself, if this is at all convenient. Not only can you then inspect the snakes before you purchase them, you can ensure they have a comfortable journey home. If travelling by car on a short journey in reasonably warm weather, it is usually quite okay to put the snake in its bag on the floor of the car. For longer or colder journeys, you should place the bag(s) into a box or boxes.

When sending snakes by public transport or freightline, ensure that each individual bag is labelled, that the transport box is insulated, and that it is clearly marked with the name, address and telephone number of the consignee, plus instructions to the effect that the crate should not be left outside in cold conditions.

QUARANTINE

A whole disease epidemic among your pets could be started by a newcomer if you do not take precautions. Even with careful inspection at the time of purchase, it is always easy to miss something, especially if it is a disease in its early stages and not yet showing symptoms. That is why it is important for all newly acquired snakes to be given a period of isolated quarantine before you introduce them to any existing snakes you may have.

All newcomers should be housed in a heated quarantine cage with minimum furnishings (a water bath, a hidebox, and absorbent paper substrate being sufficient), and kept under close observation for not less than 28 days. Quarantine cages should be kept in a completely different room from the one in which your main stock is kept and you should maintain strict hygienic conditions, ensuring that you do not transmit germs from your new snakes to your existing stock. Always wash your hands thoroughly between each handling/cleaning session.

If no disease symptoms appear during the quarantine period, you can safely assume that the snake is healthy and you can transfer it to more normal accommodations. If you notice anything suspect or are not sure, however, you should get advice from your veterinarian, or from a more experienced enthusiast, before taking the snake out of quarantine.

HANDLING AND TAMING

It is necessary to handle your snakes frequently and regularly in order to tame them, to keep them tame, and at the same time to inspect them. Although Ball Pythons are normally docile and will make no attempt to bite, if they are not tame they will do the "ball

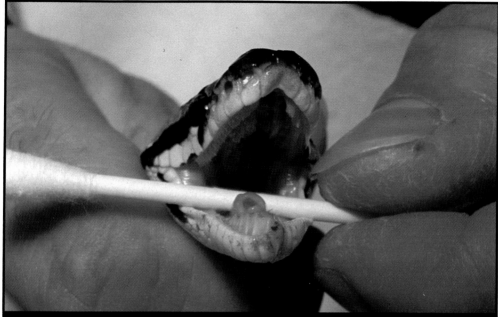

Whenever you have to work around a snake's mouth (in order to apply ointments, to force-feed, or whatever), be firm but gentle, and only use soft items like this cotton swab. Using something like the handle of a stainless steel spoon or a fountain pen can cause oral damage to the snake.

trick" and remain relatively uninteresting. A young Ball Python can usually be picked up with one hand in the middle of its body and allowed to twine itself around your fingers. Young snakes, the younger the better, are the easiest to tame and will usually become quite comfortable in your hand after a few sessions, often staying for hours just crawling through your fingers and tasting them with the tongue. The tasting is obviously not a prelude to feeding in this case but perhaps just an example of the snake reassuring itself. A larger Ball Python should be picked up gently but firmly with both hands roughly one-third and two-thirds along its body; it can then be draped over the arms and restrained occasionally if it tries to crawl off.

Hand-reared Ball Pythons will usually remain tame as long as they are handled frequently. Indeed, they seem to enjoy the handling sessions; maybe it is the warmth of the human body they get to like. Whatever it is, many enthusiasts build up a friendly rapport with their pythons which is certainly good for all involved.

TW-128, 592 pgs, 1400+ color photos

TS-144, 208 pgs, 200+ photos & illus.

TS-194, 192 pgs, 175+ photos

TS-193, 736 pgs, 1400+ color photos

TS-189, 224 pgs, 180+ color photos

KW-127, 96 pgs, 80 color photos

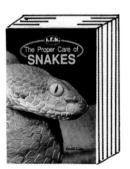

TW-111, 256 pgs, 180+ color photos

AP-925, 160 pgs, 120 photos